goSpanish

Speak & Read the Pimsleur Way

· Reading Program ·

Hear it, Learn it, Speak it, Read it

For more information, call
1-800-831-5497 or visit us
at www.Pimsleur.com

Graphic Design: Maia Kennedy

© 2002-2009 Simon & Schuster, Inc. All Rights Reserved.
Pimsleur® is an imprint of Simon & Schuster Audio, a division of Simon & Schuster, Inc.

PIMSLEUR® is a registered trademark of Beverly Pimsleur,
used by Simon & Schuster under exclusive license.
Graduated Interval Recall™ and Principle of Anticipation™ are trademarks of S&S.

*go*Spanish

*go***Spanish**

ACKNOWLEDGMENTS

VOICES
English-Speaking Instructor .... Ray Brown
Spanish-Speaking Instructor .... Eduardo Berinstein
Female Spanish Speaker............................ Stella Acelas
Male Spanish Speaker .... Jorge Drosten

WRITERS
Rudolf & Sarah Heller • Joan Schoellner

EDITORS
Christopher J. Gainty (I & II) • Elizabeth Horber (III)

EDITOR & EXECUTIVE PRODUCER
Beverly D. Heinle

PRODUCER & DIRECTOR
Sarah H. McInnis

RECORDING ENGINEERS
Peter S. Turpin • Kelly Saux

Simon & Schuster Studios, Concord, MA

*go*Spanish

TABLE OF CONTENTS

Pimsleur User's Guide 1

Introduction to the Reading Program 17

Part One 21

Part Two 55

Part Three 91

Pimsleur User's Guide *go*Spanish
Introduction

You have just purchased the most effective language program ever developed. As you probably know, learning a new language can be frustrating. Your first experience with a foreign language may have been in school. If the classes seemed difficult, or if your grades were poor, you probably believed you had no aptitude for languages. Even if you did well, you may have been surprised later to discover that what you learned was of little or no use when you tried to converse with native speakers.

Perhaps you waited until later in life and tried adult education classes, language schools, or home training programs. There too you may have found the information hard to retain, the lessons tedious, and your progress slow. Many language students give up early in these programs, convinced they lack the natural ability to understand and use what they read and hear.

The truth is that anyone can acquire a foreign language — with the right teaching system. With the Pimsleur® Method, you will benefit from the years of research and development that have helped create the world's most effective method for teaching foreign languages. The Pimsleur® Language Programs, developed by Dr. Paul Pimsleur, fill an urgent need for self-instructional materials in many languages.

Pimsleur User's Guide   *go*Spanish

How to Use the Program

To get the full benefit of each lesson, choose a quiet place where you can practice without interruption and a time of day when your mind is most alert and your body least fatigued.

The length of each lesson, just under 30 minutes, is that recommended by teaching specialists for a concentrated learning task. Once you've started the program, simply follow the tutor's instructions. The most important instruction is to respond aloud when the tutor tells you to do so. There will be a pause after this instruction, giving you time to reply. It is essential to your progress that you speak out in a normal conversational voice when asked to respond. Your active participation in thinking and speaking is required for your success in mastering this course.

The simple test for mastery is whether you are able to respond quickly and accurately when your tutor asks a question. If you are responding correctly about eighty percent of the time, then you're ready to proceed to the next lesson. It is important to keep moving forward, and also not to set unreasonable standards of perfection that will keep you from progressing, which is why we recommend using the eighty percent figure as a guide.

Pimsleur User's Guide *go*Spanish

How to Use the Program (continued)

You will notice that each lesson contains both new and familiar material, and just when you may be worrying about forgetting something, you will conveniently be reminded of it. Another helpful feature of the Pimsleur® Language Program is its rate of "saturation." You will be responding many times in the half-hour. This saturation enables you to make substantial progress within a short period of time.

Guidelines for Success

Complete the lesson units in strict consecutive order (don't skip around), doing no more than one lesson per day, although the lesson unit for the day may be repeated more than once. Daily contact with the language is critical to successful learning.

Listen carefully to each lesson unit. Always follow the directions of the tutor.

Speak out loud when directed by the tutor and answer questions within the pauses provided. It is not enough to just silently "think" of the answer to the question asked. You need to speak the answer out loud to set up a "circuit" of the language you are learning to speak so that it is heard and identified through your ears, to help to establish the "sounds"

Pimsleur User's Guide — *go*Spanish

Guidelines for Success (continued)

of the target language. Do this prior to hearing the confirmation, which is provided as reinforcement, as well as additional speech training.

Do all required activities according to the instructions, without reference to any outside persons, textbooks, or courses.

Do not have a paper and pen nearby during the lessons, and do not refer to dictionaries or other textbooks while doing the spoken lessons. The Pimsleur® Method works with the language-learning portion of your brain, requiring language to be processed in its spoken form. Not only will you interrupt the learning process if you attempt to write the words that you hear before learning to read in the new language, but you will also begin to speak the target language with an American accent. This is because the sounds represented by the American letters are frequently different from the sounds of the same-looking letters in the foreign language.

Pimsleur User's Guide   goSpanish

Dr. Paul Pimsleur

Dr. Paul Pimsleur devoted his life to language teaching and testing and was one of the world's leading experts in applied linguistics. He was fluent in French, good in German, and had a working knowledge of Italian, Russian, Modern Greek, and Mandarin Chinese. After obtaining his Ph.D. in French and a Masters in Psychology from Columbia University, he taught French Phonetics and Linguistics at UCLA. He later became Professor of Romance Languages and Language Education, and Director of The Listening Center (a state-wide language lab) at Ohio State University; Professor of Education and Romance Languages at the State University of New York at Albany; and a Fulbright lecturer at the University of Heidelberg.

Dr. Pimsleur was a founding member of the American Council on the Teaching of Foreign Languages (ACTFL). His many books and articles revolutionized theories of language learning and teaching. After years of experience and research, Dr. Pimsleur developed a new method (The Pimsleur® Method) that is based on two key principles: the *Principle of Anticipation*™ and a scientific principle of memory training that he called *Graduated Interval Recall*™. This Method has been applied to the many levels and languages of the Pimsleur® Programs.

Pimsleur User's Guide   goSpanish

Graduated Interval Recall™

Graduated Interval Recall™ is a complex name for a very simple theory about memory. No aspect of learning a foreign language is more important than memory, yet before Dr. Pimsleur, no one had explored more effective ways for building language memory.

In his research, Dr. Pimsleur discovered how long students remembered new information and at what intervals they needed to be reminded of it. If reminded too soon or too late, they failed to retain the information. This discovery enabled him to create a schedule of exactly when and how the information should be reintroduced.

Suppose you have learned a new word. You tell yourself to remember it. However, after five minutes you're unable to recall it. If you'd been reminded of it after five seconds, you probably would have remembered it for maybe a minute, at which time you would have needed another reminder. Each time you are reminded, you remember the word longer than you did the time before. The intervals between reminders become longer and longer, until you eventually remember the word without being reminded at all.

This program is carefully designed to remind you of new information at the exact intervals where maximum retention takes place. Each time your memory begins to fade, you will be asked to recall the word.

Pimsleur User's Guide goSpanish

Principle of Anticipation™

The *Principle of Anticipation*™ requires you to anticipate a correct answer. Practically, what this means is that you must retrieve the answer from what you have learned earlier in the course. It works by posing a question, asking you to provide a new sentence, using information you've learned previously and putting it into a new combination. This provides novelty and excitement which accelerates learning.

A possible scenario:

Speaker's cue: "Are you going to the movies today?"
--- PAUSE ---
Drawing on information given previously, you respond *(in the target language)*: "No, I'm going tomorrow."
The instructor will then confirm your answer:
"No, I'm going tomorrow."
The Narrator then may cue:
"Is your sister going to Europe this year?"
--- PAUSE ---
Response: "No, she went last year."

Before Dr. Pimsleur created his teaching method, language courses were based on the principle of "mindless-repetition." Teachers monotonously drummed words into the students' minds, as if there were grooves in the mind that could be worn deeper with repetition.

Pimsleur User's Guide — goSpanish

Principle of Anticipation™ (continued)

Neurophysiologists tell us however, that on the contrary, simple and unchallenging repetition has a hypnotic, even dulling effect on the learning process. Eventually, the words being repeated will lose their meaning. Dr. Pimsleur discovered that learning accelerates when there is an "input/output" system of interaction, in which students receive information and then are asked to retrieve and use it.

Core Vocabulary

While *Graduated Interval Recall*™ and the *Principle of Anticipation*™ are the foundation of the Pimsleur® Method, there are other aspects that contribute to its uniqueness and effectiveness. One involves vocabulary. We have all been intimidated, when approaching a new language, by the sheer immensity of the number of new words we must learn. But extensive research has shown that we actually need a comparatively limited number of words to be able to communicate effectively in any language.

Language can be divided into two distinct categories: grammatical structures (function words) and concrete vocabulary (content words). By focusing on the former category and enabling the student to comprehend and employ the structure of the new

Pimsleur User's Guide *go*Spanish

Core Vocabulary (continued)

language, Dr. Pimsleur found that language learners were able to more readily put new knowledge to use. There are few content words that must be known and used every day. The essential "core" of a language involves function words, which tend to relate to human activities.

This course is designed to teach you to understand and to speak the essential elements of your new language in a relatively short time. During each half-hour lesson, you will actually converse with two native speakers, using the level of language spoken by educated citizens in their everyday business and social life. The program's unique method of presenting dialogue in-situation relieves you of the most common learning problem, the problem of meaning.

Organic Learning

The Pimsleur® Method centers on teaching functional mastery in understanding and speaking a language, in the most effective and efficient way possible. You will be working on your vocabulary, grammar, and pronunciation in an integrated manner, as you are learning specific phrases that have practical use in everyday activities.

Pimsleur User's Guide goSpanish

Organic Learning (continued)

There are several thousand languages in the world. Because fewer than five hundred of these languages have developed formal systems of writing, linguistic specialists accept that language is primarily speech. For this reason, it is also accepted that the human brain acquires language as speech. Therefore, when Dr. Pimsleur created his language programs, he began teaching with recorded materials, which enabled the learners to acquire the sounds, the rhythm, and the intonation of the target language. The learners did this more rapidly, more accurately, and with great enthusiasm because they found themselves capable of almost instant beginning communication skills.

Dr. Pimsleur called this "organic learning" because it involves learning on several fronts at the same time. His system enables the learner to acquire grammatical usage, vocabulary, and the sounds of the language in an integrated, exciting way. In short, the learner gains the language as a living, expressive form of human culture.

Pimsleur User's Guide   goSpanish

"Reading" in a Pimsleur Program

A phonetic alphabet, such as the Latin alphabet and the Greek alphabet, is a list of symbols (letters) that are used to represent the sounds of the language in writing. And given that language is primarily speech, the spoken sounds of the language necessarily precede learning how to decode the written form, i.e., learning how to "read" – just as a child first learns to speak and then eventually to read. This is the natural progression Dr. Pimsleur followed in his courses.

After an initial introduction to the spoken language, reading is then integrated into the program and the new alphabet is systematically introduced, associating each letter with the sounds of the new language. Initially, you are sounding out words, mastering the different sounds associated with the new alphabet. You are not, at first, reading for meaning, but rather for sound/symbol correlation. Eventually, when the sound system is mastered, you will be able to look at known vocabulary and "read for meaning." By the end of the Comprehensive Level I course, you will be reading at the same level as you are speaking.

Course Content

When you have mastered a Pimsleur® Language Program, you will have a highly practical, everyday

Pimsleur User's Guide goSpanish

Course Content (continued)

vocabulary at your command. These basic words, phrases, and sentences have been carefully selected to be the most useful in everyday situations when you visit a foreign country. You will be able to handle social encounters graciously, converse with native speakers in travel situations, and use transportation systems with confidence. You'll be able to ask directions and to navigate your own way around the cities and countryside.

The language skills you learn will enable you to participate in casual conversations, express facts, give instructions, and describe current, past, and future activities. You will be able to deal with everyday survival topics and courtesy requirements. You will be intelligible to native speakers of the language — even to those who are not used to dealing with foreigners. What is equally important, you will know how to ask the kinds of questions that will further expand your knowledge of and facility with the language, because you will have been trained by the Pimsleur® open-ended questioning technique.

The Pimsleur® Method becomes a springboard for further learning and growth to take place — the ultimate purpose of any real educational system. This desire to learn will be apparent to the people with whom you speak. It will indicate sincere interest in and respect for their culture.

Pimsleur User's Guide *go*Spanish

A Note on Regional Language Differences

In any large country, and even in many smaller countries, regional differences in language are common. In the United States, for example, a person from Maine can sound very different than someone from Texas. Pronunciations ("accents") vary, and there are also minor differences in vocabulary. For example, what is called a "drinking fountain" in New York or Arizona is known as a "bubbler" in Wisconsin, and a "soft drink" in one part of America will be called a "soda" elsewhere. The differences in English are even more distinct between North Americans and Britons, or between Britons and Australians. But all are native speakers of English; all can communicate with spoken English, read the same newspapers, and watch the same television programs, essentially without difficulty.

Native speakers of a language can often tell where someone is from by listening to him or her speak. In addition to regional differences, there are social differences. Pimsleur® Language Programs use a standard "educated" speech, which will generally carry you throughout the country without difficulty.

*go*Spanish

Speak & Read the Pimsleur Way

· Reading Program ·

Introduction *go*Spanish

Pimsleur Reading Program

With *Pimsleur's Spanish Reading Program*, you will learn to read Spanish with the ease and flexibility of a native speaker. You will learn to sound out the Spanish alphabet, starting with individual words, then word combinations and short phrases, increasingly building in length until you are reading complete sentences in context. With practice, you will learn to read Spanish fluidly for meaning, and you will be able to read it aloud with near-native pronunciation.

For maximum effectiveness, we recommend that you do one or more of the spoken lessons first, before starting the Reading Lessons. Hearing the spoken sounds first will help to introduce you to the new language.

There are three parts to this Reading Program. *Part One*, the fifteen Reading Lessons from *Pimsleur's Spanish I Comprehensive Course, 2nd Revised Ed.*, will introduce you to the Spanish sound system. Since English and Spanish are both represented phonetically with the Latin alphabet, you need to learn a new, Spanish sound system. You will learn to look at the alphabet with "Spanish eyes." For example, think of the word "favor" and its pronunciation in English, compared to Spanish, "*fah - BOR.*"

Introduction   goSpanish

Pimsleur Reading Program (continued)

Although translations are provided, the meaning of the items is secondary, and we recommend you look at them only after first *reading* the sentences to sound them out with Spanish pronunciation. The items have been selected especially to give you practice in the Spanish sounds and sound combinations. Your vocabulary acquisition will begin after you've learned the Spanish sound system. You should read aloud, as directed. The process of saying the words out loud will reinforce acquisition and will help lodge the sounds in your brain. At this point you will be learning to read without an American accent.

Part Two contains the Reading Lessons from *Pimsleur's Spanish II, 3rd Ed*. This section has sixteen reading lessons that will provide practice reading letters and e-mails, numbers and times, short monologues, book titles, and selected Spanish proverbs. Translations are provided, but again, hold off on reading the translations until after you've read them using your best Spanish pronunciation. Remember to always speak aloud. Since you are working with a new sound system, you may wish to repeat some of the lessons. Do this as often as you feel necessary. If you've completed Pimsleur's Spanish II, most of the items will be familiar

Introduction   goSpanish

Pimsleur Reading Program (continued)

to you, and you'll be reading for meaning. If you haven't, then you will be learning new vocabulary, seeing and hearing it in context.

Part Three contains twenty more Reading Lessons, the Readings from *Pimsleur's Spanish III, 2nd Ed.* These lessons are intended to build your vocabulary and provide reading practice. Again, all are accompanied by translations. We still recommend, however, that you do the Reading Lessons first, sounding them out carefully before you refer to the translations. Topics covered include shopping, emergencies, restaurants and hotels, among others. In addition, you'll learn how to spell in Spanish.

All instructions for doing the Readings are contained on the audio.

goSpanish

Speak & Read the Pimsleur Way

Reading Program

PART ONE

Part One   *go*Spanish
TABLE OF CONTENTS

Reading Lessons

Lección Uno	25
Lección Dos	27
Lección Tres	29
Lección Quatro	31
Lección Cinco	33
Lección Seis	35
Lección Siete	37
Lección Ocho	39
Lección Nuevo	41
Lección Diez	43
Lección Once	45
Lección Doce	47
Lección Trece	49
Lección Catorce	51
Lección Quince	53

Part One

goSpanish

Lección Uno

1. poco
2. amigo
3. camino
4. pronto
5. calle
6. llego
7. semana
8. lleno
9. llamo
10. moreno
11. bello
12. clase
13. en la clase
14. tenemos
15. hablo
16. hasta
17. hora
18. llama
19. ¿Cómo se llama usted?
20. Hablo un poco de castellano.

Part One

*go*Spanish

Lesson One

1. little
2. friend (m.)
3. road
4. soon
5. street
6. I arrive
7. week
8. full
9. I call
10. dark-skinned / brunette
11. beautiful
12. class
13. in class
14. we have
15. I talk, speak
16. until
17. hour
18. you call / he, she calls
19. What's your name?
20. I speak a little Spanish.

Part One
Lección Dos

1. habla
2. llave
3. dinero
4. damas
5. la dama
6. delante
7. por favor
8. el papel
9. canta
10. calor
11. el señor
12. baño
13. comer
14. ella
15. la niña
16. comprar
17. entender
18. español
19. Soy de Chicago.
20. ¿Es verdad?

Part One

*go*Spanish

Lesson Two

1. you speak, talk / he, she speaks, talks
2. key
3. money
4. ladies
5. the lady
6. in front
7. please
8. the paper
9. you sing / he, she sings
10. heat
11. Mr. / sir
12. bathroom
13. to eat
14. she / her
15. the girl
16. to buy
17. to understand
18. Spanish
19. I'm from Chicago.
20. Really?

Part One

*go*Spanish

Lección Tres

1. usted / Ud.
2. Norteamérica
3. ¿Es usted de Norteamérica?
4. Sí, soy norteamericano.
5. No hablo español.
6. entiendo
7. muy bien
8. ¿Entiende?
9. ¿Entiende usted?
10. ¿Dónde?
11. saber
12. norte
13. norteamericana
14. bañar
15. lloro
16. ¿Habla español, señorita?
17. No importa.
18. Estamos en Chile.
19. Está bien.
20. Adiós.

Part One

goSpanish

Lesson Three

1. you
2. North America
3. Are you from North America?
4. Yes, I'm North American (m.)
5. I don't speak Spanish.
6. I understand
7. very well
8. (Do you) understand?
9. Do *you* understand?
10. Where?
11. to know
12. north
13. North American (f.)
14. to shower / to bathe
15. I cry
16. Do you speak Spanish, miss?
17. It doesn't matter.
18. We're in Chile.
19. That's OK / fine.
20. Good-bye.

Part One — *go*Spanish
Lección Quatro

1. año
2. las horas
3. el año
4. la tarde
5. ellos
6. bueno
7. Buenas noches.
8. grande
9. casa
10. la casa grande
11. hambre
12. hombre
13. Perdón.
14. puerta
15. puedo
16. dueño
17. el pollo
18. dos helados

Part One **goSpanish**

Lesson Four
● ●

1. year
2. the hours
3. the year
4. the afternoon
5. they (m.)
6. good
7. Good evening. / Good night.
8. big / large
9. house
10. the big house
11. hunger
12. man
13. Excuse me.
14. door
15. I can
16. owner
17. the chicken
18. two ice cream cones

Part One
goSpanish
Lección Cinco

1. quiero
2. quema
3. frase
4. aquello
5. libra
6. está
7. esta
8. aquí
9. Está allí.
10. No está allí, señora.
11. habrá
12. quedo
13. quien
14. No tengo dólares.
15. ¿Dónde está el Hotel Colón?
16. Está a dos calles de aquí.
17. ¿Qué le ha dicho?
18. No me ha dicho nada.

Part One
Lesson Five

1. I want
2. it burns
3. phrase
4. that (m.)
5. pound
6. you are / (he, she, it) is
7. this (f.)
8. here
9. It's there.
10. It's not there, ma'am.
11. there will be
12. I stay, remain / quiet
13. who
14. I don't have (any) dollars.
15. Where is the Columbus Hotel?
16. It's two blocks from here.
17. What has (he, she) told you?
18. He, She hasn't told me anything.

Part One

goSpanish

Lección Seis

1. Buenos días.
2. mucho
3. muchacho
4. mañana
5. No quiero.
6. ¿Cuántos pesos quiere?
7. ¿Cómo está usted, señor García?
8. una palabra
9. dos palabras
10. ¡Es maravilloso!
11. mi madre
12. gente
13. gitano
14. un gran gitano
15. lejos
16. Juan
17. Jorge
18. Tengo un gato.
19. la geografía
20. José es mi hermano.

Part One

goSpanish

Lesson Six

1. Good morning.
2. much (m.)
3. boy / young man
4. tomorrow
5. I don't want (to / any).
6. How many pesos do you / does he, she want?
7. How are you, Mr. García?
8. a / one word
9. two words
10. It's marvelous!
11. my mother
12. people
13. gypsy
14. a great gypsy
15. far (away)
16. John
17. George
18. I have a cat.
19. the geography
20. Joseph is my brother.

Part One

goSpanish

Lección Siete

1. Esa mujer ---
2. es de Argentina.
3. ¡Quiero beber champaña!
4. Hoy es jueves.
5. Ese caballero ---
6. es mi sobrino.
7. En el mes de septiembre ---
8. empieza el otoño.
9. ¿Donde está el general?
10. Es un gigante.
11. jugar
12. No quiero jugar.
13. azul
14. Es el número cinco.
15. en el mes de marzo
16. dos cervezas
17. la página
18. el guiso
19. la guerra
20. ¡Qué horror!

Part One

Lesson Seven

goSpanish

1. That woman ---
2. is from Argentina.
3. I want to drink champagne!
4. Today is Thursday.
5. That gentleman ---
6. is my nephew.
7. In the month of September ---
8. autumn starts.
9. Where is the general?
10. He's a giant.
11. to play
12. I don't want to play.
13. blue
14. It's number five.
15. in the month of March
16. two beers
17. the page
18. the stew
19. the war
20. How awful!

Part One

goSpanish

Lección Ocho

1. correspondencia
2. el cielo cubierto
3. pague
4. llegue
5. Llegó a las diez y media.
6. ¿Hay tiempo?
7. ¿No te gusta la cerveza?
8. Quiero agua fría.
9. Es una zona comercial.
10. Cuidado con el perro.
11. La señora me llama.
12. Se llama Jiménez.
13. Toca la guitarra.
14. enseguida
15. ¡Qué cabeza!
16. ¡Me hace daño!
17. ¿De dónde es el señor Gómez?
18. Es de Guatemala.

Part One

goSpanish

Lesson Eight

1. correspondence
2. the covered sky
3. you pay
4. I arrive / he, she, it arrives (subjunctive)
5. You, He, She, It arrived at ten thirty.
6. Is there time?
7. Don't you like beer?
8. I want cold water.
9. It's a commercial / business area.
10. Beware of the dog.
11. The lady is calling me.
12. Her, His name is Jiménez.
13. He, She plays the guitar.
14. at once / immediately
15. What a head!
16. It hurts me!
17. From where is Mr. Gómez?
18. He's from Guatemala.

Part One   goSpanish
Lección Nuevo

1. ¡Vamos!
2. barco
3. vivido / bebido
4. Me gusta viajar en barco.
5. Los bandidos se van.
6. ¿Quién va a pagar?
7. según el libro
8. saco / saque
9. la cuenta
10. nueve / jueves
11. llueve
12. el pájaro
13. Julio lo dijo.
14. ¡Qué sonrisa!
15. No creo que lleguen.
16. Voy a beber tres cervezas ---
17. en cuatro minutos.
18. ¿Conoce a Jorge?
19. Sí, lo conozco.
20. Pero no sé dónde está.

Part One

goSpanish

Lesson Nine

1. Let's go!
2. boat
3. lived / drank
4. I like traveling / to travel by boat.
5. The bandits are leaving.
6. Who is going to pay?
7. according to the book
8. sack, jacket, I take out (present tense or subjunctive) / he, she takes out (subjunctive)
9. the check / bill
10. nine / Thursday
11. it rains
12. the bird
13. Julio said that.
14. What a smile!
15. I don't think that they will arrive.
16. I'm going to drink three beers ---
17. in four minutes.
18. Do you know George?
19. Yes, I know him.
20. But I don't know where he is.

Part One
goSpanish
Lección Diez

1. la ley
2. seguir
3. No hay nada.
4. ¿Qué hay allí?
5. Hay muchas cosas.
6. Vamos a comer ahora.
7. Apáguela.
8. Apague la luz.
9. A las cuatro menos cuarto.
10. el número dieciséis
11. ¡Hola, José!
12. Dígame, ¿qué hora es?
13. Ahora son las doce.
14. No entiendo muy bien.
15. ¿Dónde está su esposa?
16. Mi esposa está en México.
17. Habla demasiado despacio.
18. ¿De veras?

Part One

*go*Spanish

Lesson Ten

1. the law
2. to continue
3. There is nothing.
4. What's there?
5. There are many things.
6. Let's go eat now. / We're going to eat now.
7. Turn it off.
8. Turn off the light.
9. At quarter to four.
10. the number sixteen
11. Hi / Hello, Joseph!
12. Tell me, what time is it?
13. Now it's twelve (o'clock).
14. I don't understand very well.
15. Where's your wife?
16. My wife is in Mexico.
17. You speak / He, She speaks too slowly.
18. Really?

Part One
Lección Once

1. ¿Qué va a beber?
2. Voy a tomar café.
3. Puedo beberlo, pero no puedo pagarlo.
4. Hoy no tengo dinero.
5. Yo tengo muchos pesos.
6. veinticinco
7. treinta y ocho
8. cuarenta y nueve
9. ¿Qué va a hacer?
10. Nosotros no sabemos.
11. No sabemos qué vamos a comprar.
12. Pero queremos comprar algo.
13. Porque tenemos pesos ---
14. y dólares también.
15. ¡Qué noche más bella!
16. Al día siguiente ---
17. llegué a Los Ángeles.
18. Siga por allí.

Part One

Lesson Eleven — *goSpanish*

1. What are you going to drink?
2. I'm going to have coffee.
3. I can drink it, but I can't pay for it.
4. Today I don't have (any) money.
5. *I* have a lot of pesos.
6. twenty-five
7. thirty-eight
8. forty-nine
9. What are you / is he, she going to do?
10. *We* don't know.
11. We don't know what we're going to buy.
12. But we want to buy something.
13. Because we have pesos ---
14. and dollars also.
15. What a beautiful night!
16. The next day ---
17. I arrived in Los Angeles.
18. Continue / Go on that way.

Part One

goSpanish

Lección Doce

1. Tiene la boca abierta.
2. Se acuesta temprano.
3. Ella queda contenta.
4. No hay ni escuela ni teatro.
5. Nos fuimos después.
6. Vivía con Juanito.
7. Quiso pegarme.
8. No, no es nuestro amigo.
9. ¿Está en España?
10. No sé, quizás.
11. Creo que sí.
12. Me voy a las once y cuarto.
13. Mis amigos están listos.
14. Se van ahora.
15. Roberto, ¿dónde estás?
16. Cerró la puerta.
17. Pero, ¿dónde está el perro?
18. Es aquélla, la roja.

Part One

Lesson Twelve

1. You have your mouth open. / He, She has his, her mouth open.
2. You go / He, She goes to bed early.
3. She remains happy.
4. There's neither (a) school nor (a) theater.
5. We left afterwards.
6. He, She lived with Johnny.
7. He, She wanted to hit me.
8. No, he's not our friend.
9. Is he, she in Spain?
10. I don't know, maybe.
11. I think so.
12. I'll leave / I'm leaving at quarter past eleven.
13. My friends are ready.
14. They're leaving now.
15. Robert, where are you?
16. He, She closed the door.
17. But, where's the dog?
18. It's that one, the red one (f.).

Part One   **goSpanish**

Lección Trece

1. Estamos listos, ¿verdad?
2. Sí, pero no hay tiempo para comer.
3. ¿Quiere una copa de vino blanco?
4. los números dieciocho y veinte
5. ¿Quién tiene dinero?
6. Todos mis amigos tienen dinero.
7. ¿Puede ayudarme?
8. La música es malagueña.
9. Esta persona habla muy rápido.
10. Este hombre habla despacio, ¿verdad?
11. Déme un vaso de agua.
12. ¿Qué quiere decir esa palabra?
13. Siga derecho; el hotel está a la izquierda.
14. ¿Cuál es la dirección de su amigo?
15. Te lo he dicho, ¿no te acuerdas?
16. Lo siento. No me acuerdo de eso.
17. Esta película es excelente.
18. El cine está a sólo cinco cuadras de mi casa.

Part One

*go*Spanish

Lesson Thirteen

1. We're ready, aren't we?
2. Yes, but there's no time to eat.
3. Do you / Does he, she want a glass of white wine?
4. the numbers eighteen and twenty
5. Who has money?
6. All my friends have money.
7. Can you help me?
8. The music is from Malaga.
9. This person speaks very fast.
10. This man speaks slowly, doesn't he?
11. Give me a glass of water.
12. What does that word mean?
13. Continue straight ahead; the hotel is on the left.
14. What's your friend's address?
15. I've told you, don't you remember?
16. I'm sorry. I don't remember that.
17. This film is excellent.
18. The movie theater is only five blocks from my house.

Part One

*go*Spanish

Lección Catorce

1. Venga conmigo a mi casa.
2. ¿Me ha entendido? No, no le he entendido.
3. Ya lo he dicho dos veces, pero voy a decirlo otra vez.
4. Mi padre es profesor; vive en España.
5. La ciudad de Santiago está en Chile.
6. No hemos podido hablar con la gente de la región.
7. ¿Cuánto es quince más tres?
8. Dieciocho, ¿no lo sabes?
9. Cuando mi hijo era pequeño, siempre estaba enfermo.
10. Me ha dicho un amigo que hace buen tiempo allí.
11. Usted no sabe la dirección, pero yo la sé.
12. Voy a dársela. Escríbala.
13. Esa película nos gusta mucho.
14. La hemos visto tres veces.
15. Ustedes han bebido mucho, ¿verdad?
16. Y ¿qué tal? ¿Cómo están ustedes?
17. No me ha contestado todavía.
18. Ya hemos comido. No necesitamos nada.

Part One

*go*Spanish

Lesson Fourteen

1. Come home with me.
2. Have you understood me? No, I haven't understood you.
3. I've said it twice already, but I'm going to say it again.
4. My father is a professor / teacher; he lives in Spain.
5. The city of Santiago is in Chile.
6. We haven't been able to talk with the people of the region.
7. How much is fifteen plus three?
8. Eighteen, don't you know?
9. When my son was little, he was always sick.
10. A friend has told me that the weather is good there.
11. You don't know the address, but *I* know it.
12. I'm going to give it to you. Write it down.
13. We like that movie very much.
14. We've seen it three times.
15. You have drunk a lot, haven't you?
16. So how's it going? How are you?
17. You haven't / He, She hasn't answered me yet.
18. We've eaten already. We don't need anything.

Part One

*go*Spanish

Lección Quince

1. ¡Espere un momentito!
2. Voy a acompañarle.
3. Lo que ha dicho no es interesante.
4. Es un sistema característico y normal.
5. A la mañana siguiente, cuando llegué ---
6. no estaba allí.
7. El médico ha hablado usando muchas palabras latinas.
8. El accidente pasó en el mes de octubre.
9. Tengo que irme ahora. Hasta luego.
10. Cuando se fue me quedé llorando.
11. La ciudad está demasiado lejos;
12. no podemos llegar allí.
13. No me ha gustado ese trabajo.
14. Los hombres con barba tal vez tienen un aspecto bárbaro.
15. No hay ninguna persona en la escuela.
16. Las mujeres han disfrutado la comida.
17. Dicen que la vida es sueño.
18. Déme la dirección de su casa, por favor.

Part One   goSpanish

Lesson Fifteen

1. Wait a minute!
2. I'm going with you.
3. What you have said / he, she has said is not interesting.
4. It's a characteristic and normal system.
5. The next day, when I arrived ---
6. he, she wasn't there / you weren't there.
7. The doctor has spoken using many Latin words.
8. The accident happened in the month of October.
9. I have to leave now. So long.
10. When he, she, you left, I stayed behind crying.
11. The city is too far away;
12. we can't get there.
13. I didn't like that job.
14. Men with beards have the aspect of a barbarian.
15. There's not one person in the school.
16. The women have enjoyed the meal.
17. They say that life is a dream.
18. Give me your, his, her home address, please.

*go*Spanish
Speak & Read the Pimsleur Way

· Reading Program ·

PART TWO

Part Two — goSpanish

TABLE OF CONTENTS

Reading Lessons

Lección Uno: Un viaje a Honduras	59
Lección Dos: Pida instrucciones para llegar	61
Lección Tres: Planes para la tarde	63
Lección Cuatro: Una invitación informal	65
Lección Cinco: Una carta	67
Lección Seis: Un mensaje de correo electrónico	69
Lección Siete: Vacaciones	71
Lección Ocho: El dinero	73
Lección Nueve: Los números	75
Lección Diez: La hora	77
Lección Once: Algunos usos de "tener"	79
Lección Doce: Mucho que hacer	81
Lección Trece: El béisbol	83
Lección Catorce: Los títulos de algunos cuentos populares	85
Lección Quince: Unos refranes comunes	87
Lección Dieciséis: Más refranes comunes	89

Part Two *go*Spanish

Lección Uno - Un viaje a Honduras

1. Quiero hacer un viaje.
2. ¿Conoces Honduras?
3. No. No he estado allí.
4. Es un país en América Latina.
5. No es muy grande ---
6. pero es muy bonito.
7. En verano hace mucho calor ---
8. pero ahora hace buen tiempo.
9. También hay mucha gente buena.
10. Pero no conozco a nadie.
11. Prefiero conocer a alguien.
12. La gente habla demasiado rápido.
13. No entiendo nada.
14. ¡Sí, entiendes mucho!

Part Two

*go*Spanish

Lesson One - A Trip to Honduras

1. I want to take a trip.
2. Do you know / Have you been to Honduras?
3. No. I haven't been there.
4. It's a country in Latin America.
5. It's not very big ---
6. but it's very beautiful.
7. In the summer it's very hot ---
8. but now the weather's nice.
9. There are also many nice people.
10. But I don't know anyone.
11. I would prefer to know someone.
12. People speak too fast.
13. I don't understand anything.
14. Yes, you understand a lot!

Part Two   *go*Spanish

Lección Dos - Pida instrucciones para llegar

1. El hombre exclamó: "¡Perdón!"
2. Entonces preguntó: "¿Podría ayudarme?"
3. Creo que estoy perdido.
4. Busco la calle Juárez.
5. Pero no puedo encontrarla.
6. Tengo un mapa.
7. ¿Podría mostrarme en el mapa ---
8. dónde queda esta calle?
9. Cómo no.
10. No necesita el mapa.
11. La calle Juárez queda a sólo tres cuadras de aquí ---
12. a la derecha.
13. Muchas gracias, señorita.
14. A sus órdenes.

Part Two *go*Spanish

Lesson Two - Asking Directions

1. The man exclaimed: "Sorry!"
2. Then he asked: "Could you help me?"
3. I think I'm lost.
4. I'm looking for Juarez Street.
5. But I can't find it.
6. I have a map.
7. Could you show me in the map ---
8. where this street is?
9. Sure. / Of course.
10. You don't need a map.
11. Juarez Street is only three blocks from here ---
12. to the right.
13. Thanks a lot, miss.
14. You're welcome. / It's a pleasure.

Part Two　　　　　　　　　　　　　　*go***Spanish**

Lección Tres - Planes para la tarde

1. Vamos a una película boliviana.
2. Comienza temprano.
3. A las cuatro y cuarto.
4. Después, vamos a ver a una señora.
5. Ella es buena amiga mía.
6. Es muy simpática.
7. Escribe libros para niños.
8. Tiene un hijo y una hija.
9. Ellos tienen un gatito pequeñito.
10. Pero quieren un perro grande.
11. Los niños estudian en el Colegio Bolívar.
12. El colegio comienza en septiembre.
13. ¿Dónde vive esta amiga suya?
14. En la Avenida Buena Vista. No queda lejos.
15. Y después de visitarla, podemos ir al restaurante.
16. Buena idea. ¡Vamos!

Part Two — *go*Spanish

Lesson Three - Afternoon Plans

1. We're going to (see) a Bolivian movie.
2. It starts early.
3. At quarter past four.
4. Afterwards, we're going to visit / to see a woman.
5. She's a good friend of mine.
6. She's very nice.
7. She writes children's books.
8. She has a son and a daughter.
9. They have a small kitten.
10. But they want a big dog.
11. The children study at the Bolivar School.
12. School starts in September.
13. Where does this friend of yours live?
14. On Buena Vista Avenue. It's not far.
15. And after we visit her, we can go to the restaurant.
16. Good idea. Let's go!

Part Two — goSpanish

Lección Cuatro - Una invitación informal

1. ¡Hola, María Elena!
2. Mañana jueves hay una fiesta.
3. Es para un amigo de Los Ángeles.
4. ¿Conoces a Roberto, mi amigo norteamericano?
5. Él se va pasado mañana.
6. ¿Puedes ir a la fiesta con nosotros?
7. Es en un restaurante.
8. Se llama *El Gaucho Gigante*.
9. Comienza a las nueve.
10. Pero Roberto llega a las nueve y media.
11. Es una sorpresa ---
12. así que no digas nada a nadie.
13. Puedes invitar a tu hermana también.
14. Llámame, por favor. --- Jorge

Part Two

goSpanish

Lesson Four - An Informal Invitation

1. Hello / Hi, Mary Ellen!
2. Tomorrow, Thursday, there's a party.
3. It's for a friend from Los Angeles.
4. Do you know Robert, my North American friend?
5. He's leaving the day after tomorrow.
6. Can you go to the party with us?
7. It's in a restaurant.
8. Its name is *The Giant Gaucho*.
9. It starts at nine (o'clock).
10. But Robert will be arriving at nine-thirty.
11. It's a surprise ---
12. so don't say anything to anyone.
13. You can invite your sister too.
14. Call me, please. --- George

Part Two *go*Spanish

Lección Cinco - Una carta

1. Querida Familia Dueñas:
2. ¿Cómo están Ustedes? / ¿Uds.?
3. Yo estoy muy bien.
4. Escribo esta carta desde Brasil.
5. Estoy aquí en un viaje de negocios.
6. Me quedo en Rio de Janiero ---
7. hasta el miércoles entrante.
8. Después voy a Buenos Aires.
9. Si tengo suficiente tiempo, ---
10. quiero salir de la ciudad un poco.
11. También me gustaría ---
12. conocer las Pampas.
13. Pero entonces necesitaré alquilar un coche.
14. Sin coche es difícil.
15. ¡Saludos a todos!
16. Su amigo, Bill Jameson

Part Two

goSpanish

Lesson Five - A Letter

1. Dear Dueñas Family,
2. How are (all of) you?
3. I'm very well.
4. I'm writing this letter from Brazil.
5. I'm here on a business trip.
6. I'm staying in Rio de Janeiro ---
7. until next Wednesday.
8. Then I'm going to Buenos Aires.
9. If I have enough time, ---
10. I want to get out of the city for a little (while).
11. I would also like ---
12. to visit / to know the Pampas.
13. But then I would need to rent a car.
14. Without a car, it's difficult.
15. Regards to everyone!
16. Your friend, Bill Jameson

Part Two — *go*Spanish

Lección Seis - Un mensaje de correo electrónico

1. Mensaje para José Duarte:
2. ¡Perdón! No he podido contestarte antes.
3. Aquí hay demasiado trabajo.
4. Salgo para Madrid el lunes entrante.
5. ¿Podemos encontrarnos allí?
6. Quizás el martes a la una.
7. Podríamos almorzar juntos.
8. Hay varias cosas importantes para hablar.
9. Contéstame cuanto antes.
10. Prometo contestar el mismo día.
11. Y ¿cómo va ese proyecto grande?
12. ¿Hay algo nuevo?
13. Saludos a tu esposa.
14. Hasta pronto. --- Franco

Part Two

*go*Spanish

Lesson Six - An E-mail Message

1. Message for Joseph Duarte:
2. I'm sorry! I haven't been able to answer you before (this).
3. Here there's too much work.
4. I'm leaving for Madrid this coming Monday.
5. Can we meet there?
6. Maybe Tuesday at one (o'clock).
7. We could have lunch together.
8. There are several important things to talk about.
9. Answer me as soon as possible.
10. I promise to reply the same day.
11. And how's that big project going?
12. Is there anything new?
13. Regards to your wife.
14. See you soon. --- Frank

Part Two

*go*Spanish

Lección Siete - Vacaciones

1. Necesitamos hacer una reservación.
2. Hay que llegar al hotel antes de las nueve.
3. El restaurante está abierto hasta las once.
4. El vino es bueno.
5. Sí, y la comida también.
6. Pero es cara.
7. Y ¿qué quiere hacer mañana?
8. Si llueve, me gustaría ir al museo.
9. Si hace buen tiempo ---
10. vamos a la playa.
11. A los niños les gusta mucho la playa.
12. ¿Cómo llegamos?
13. Podemos ir en autobús, o en taxi.
14. El taxi es más rápido y más cómodo.
15. ¡Van a ser vacaciones caras!
16. Lo sé.

Part Two

goSpanish

Lesson Seven - Vacations

1. We need to make a reservation.
2. We have to arrive at the hotel before nine (o'clock).
3. The restaurant is open until eleven (o'clock).
4. The wine is good.
5. Yes, and the food, too.
6. But it's expensive.
7. And what do you want to do tomorrow?
8. If it rains, I'd like to go the museum.
9. If it's good weather ---
10. let's go to the beach.
11. The children like the beach a lot.
12. How do we get there?
13. We can go by bus, or by taxi.
14. A taxi is faster and more comfortable.
15. This is going to be an expensive vacation!
16. I know it.

Part Two   goSpanish

Lección Ocho - El dinero

1. En los Estados Unidos usan dólares.
2. "Estados Unidos" se abrevia: EE.UU.
3. En Canadá, también usan dólares.
4. Son dólares canadienses.
5. Cien centavos son un dólar.
6. En muchos países usan pesos.
7. En algunos países de América Latina ---
8. usan el punto decimal.
9. En otros países usan la coma decimal.
10. ¿Cuánto cuesta todo junto?
11. Déjeme ver ---
12. dos mil trescientos cincuenta pesos.
13. O doscientos trece dólares.
14. Es muy caro.
15. Puede pagar con tarjeta de crédito.
16. Porque no tengo mucho dinero.

Part Two — goSpanish

Lesson Eight - Money

1. In the United States they use dollars.
2. "United States" is abbreviated: U.S.
3. In Canada, they also use dollars.
4. They're Canadian dollars.
5. One hundred cents are a dollar.
6. In many countries they use pesos.
7. In some countries of Latin America ---
8. they use the decimal point.
9. In other countries they use the decimal comma.
10. How much does it cost altogether?
11. Let me see ---
12. two thousand three hundred fifty pesos.
13. Or two hundred thirteen dollars.
14. It's very expensive.
15. You can pay with credit card.
16. Because I don't have much money.

Part Two
*go*Spanish

Lección Nueve - Los números

1. Uno y uno son dos.
2. Tres y cuatro son siete.
3. Seis menos seis son cero.
4. Ocho menos siete son uno.
5. Nueve por dos son dieciocho.
6. Seis por siete son cuarenta y dos.
7. Setenta y dos dividido en ocho son nueve.
8. Cincuenta dividido en dos son veinticinco.
9. Siete y ocho son quince.
10. Cien y cien son doscientos.
11. Diez mil menos nueve mil son mil.
12. Catorce menos tres son once.
13. Cuatro por cinco son veinte.
14. Dos por tres son seis.
15. Treinta y dos dividido en cuatro son ocho.
16. Sesenta y tres dividido en siete son nueve.

Part Two

*go*Spanish

Lesson Nine - Numbers

1. One and one are two.
2. Three and four are seven.
3. Six minus six is zero.
4. Eight minus seven is one.
5. Nine times two is eighteen.
6. Six times seven is forty-two.
7. Seventy-two divided by eight is nine.
8. Fifty divided by two is twenty-five.
9. Seven and eight are fifteen.
10. One hundred and one hundred are two hundred.
11. Ten thousand minus nine thousand is one thousand.
12. Fourteen minus three is eleven.
13. Four times five is twenty.
14. Two times three is six.
15. Thirty-two divided by four is eight.
16. Sixty-three divided by seven is nine.

Part Two
*go*Spanish
Lección Diez - La hora

1. ¿Qué hora es?
2. Es la hora del almuerzo.
3. Al mediodía, son las doce del día.
4. Son las doce de la noche --- la medianoche.
5. Es la una y cinco de la tarde.
6. Va a ser la una y cuarto.
7. El avión sale a las siete y media.
8. Llega mañana en la mañana.
9. ¿A qué hora tengo que estar lista?
10. A las seis y cuarto.
11. El metro llega cada quince minutos.
12. ¿Cuánto tiempo para llegar?
13. Más o menos un cuarto de hora.
14. Vamos a las cinco menos cuarto.
15. Siempre llega tarde.
16. El concierto comienza en media hora.
17. Si comienza a tiempo.
18. Ahora, son las tres en punto.

Part Two   *go*Spanish

Lesson Ten - Time
• •

1. What time is it?
2. It's lunchtime.
3. At noon, it's twelve (in the daytime).
4. It's twelve at night --- midnight.
5. It's five past one in the afternoon.
6. It's close to / It's going to be a quarter past one.
7. The plane leaves at seven-thirty.
8. It arrives tomorrow morning.
9. (At) what time do I have to be ready?
10. At a quarter past six.
11. The subway arrives every fifteen minutes.
12. How long does it take to get there?
13. More or less a quarter of an hour.
14. Let's go / We'll go at a quarter to five.
15. He, She always arrives late. / You always arrive late.
16. The concert starts in half an hour.
17. If it starts on time.
18. Now, it's three on the dot.

Part Two — *go*Spanish

Lección Once - Algunos usos de "tener"

1. Hay que tener valor.
2. El profesor tiene una buena idea.
3. ¿Tiene usted hambre?
4. No, pero tengo sed.
5. Mi padre tiene sueño.
6. Los niños tienen prisa de salir.
7. ¿Cuántos años tiene usted?
8. Tengo dolor de cabeza.
9. Hay que tener cuidado hoy.
10. Tiene ganas de venir a mi casa?
11. Creo que estoy enfermo, porque tengo mucho frío.
12. ¿Tiene tiempo para ir al cine?
13. Tengo que escribir una carta.
14. Esta mañana no tengo suerte.

Part Two   goSpanish

Lesson Eleven - Some Expressions Using "Have"

1. One has to have courage.
2. The professor has a good idea.
3. Are you hungry?
   Literal translation: *Do you have hunger?*
4. No, but I'm thirsty.
   Literal translation: *No, but I have thirst.*
5. My father is sleepy.
   Literal translation: *My father has sleepiness.*
6. The children are in a hurry to go out.
   Literal trans.: *The children have haste to go out.*
7. How old are you?
   Literal trans.: *How many years do you have?*
8. I have a headache.
9. It's necessary to be careful today.
   Literal trans.: *It's necesary to have care today.*
10. Would you like to come to my house?
    Literal: *Do you have cravings to come to my house?*
11. I think I'm sick, because I'm very cold.
    Literal translation: *... because I have a lot of cold.*
12. Do you have time to go to the movies?
13. I have to write a letter.
14. This morning I don't have any luck.

Part Two — *go*Spanish

Lección Doce - Mucho que hacer

1. ¿Cuándo quiere jugar al tenis la semana entrante?
2. ¿Qué tal el lunes?
3. No, el lunes voy a visitar a mi padre.
4. No lo he visto desde hace la semana pasada.
5. ¿Entonces el martes?
6. No, no puedo el martes tampoco.
7. El martes tengo una reunión importante en el banco.
8. Bueno, ¿el miércoles?
9. El miércoles voy al cine con una amiga.
10. ¿El jueves? ¿O el viernes?
11. Lo siento mucho, pero el jueves ---
12. tengo que llevar mi madre al médico.
13. Su coche no funciona ahora.
14. Y el viernes tengo que comprar unas cosas.
15. ¿Quizás el fin de semana?
16. ¡El fin de semana tengo que trabajar!

Part Two *go*Spanish

Lesson Twelve - A Lot to Do

1. When do you want to play tennis next week?
2. What about Monday?
3. No, Monday I'm going to visit my father.
4. I haven't seen him since last week.
5. Then on Tuesday?
6. No, I can't on Tuesday either.
7. Tuesday I have an important meeting at the bank.
8. Fine, on Wednesday?
9. On Wednesday I'm going to the movies with a (girl)friend.
10. Thursday? Or Friday?
11. I'm very sorry, but on Thursday ---
12. I have to take my mother to the doctor.
13. Her car isn't working now.
14. And Friday I have to buy some things.
15. Maybe the weekend?
16. On the weekend I have to work!

Part Two — *go*Spanish

Lección Trece - El béisbol

1. Me gusta jugar al béisbol.
2. También me gusta mirarlo.
3. El puertorriqueño que juega tan bien es de San Juan.
4. Sólo tiene veintidós años.
5. Pero en el estadio, los asientos no son cómodos.
6. A veces los perros calientes están fríos.
7. Con frecuencia, llueve o hace demasiado calor.
8. Podemos verlo en televisión.
9. ¿Quiere venir a mi casa?
10. ¡Ojalá que sí!
11. Puede llamarme esta noche.
12. Mi número de teléfono es el ---
13. Seis - treinta y ocho - quince - cuarenta y siete.
14. ¡Hasta luego!

Part Two

goSpanish

Lesson Thirteen - Baseball

1. I like to play baseball.
2. I also like to watch it.
3. The Puerto Rican who plays so well is from San Juan.
4. He's only twenty-two years (old).
5. But in the stadium, the seats are not comfortable.
6. Sometimes the hot dogs are cold.
7. Frequently, it rains or it's too hot.
8. We can watch it on television.
9. Do you want to come to my house?
10. I hope so!
11. You can call me tonight.
12. My telephone number is ---
13. Six – thirty-eight – fifteen – forty-seven.
14. So long!

Part Two   goSpanish

Lección Catorce - Los títulos de algunos cuentos populares

1. Platero y yo
   English Title: *Platero and I*
   Author: Juan Ramón Jiménez, Spaniard

2. El mal del tiempo
   English Title: *Restless*
   Author: Carlos Fuentes, Mexican

3. El gaucho Martín Fierro
   English Title: *The Gaucho Martin Fierro*
   Author: José Hernandez, Argentinian

4. Cien años de soledad
   English Title: *One Hundred Years of Solitude*
   Author: Gabriel García Márquez, Colombian

5. El ingenioso hidalgo Don Quijote de la Mancha
   English Title: Don Quixote
   Literal: *The Ingenious Gentleman / Nobleman Don Quixote of La Mancha*
   Author: Miguel de Cervantes Saavedra, Spaniard

6. Cuando era puertorriqueña
   English Title: *When I was Puerto Rican*
   Author: Esmeralda Santiago, Puerto Rican

Part Two   *go*Spanish

Lesson Fourteen - Titles of Some Popular Stories

7. Como agua para chocolate
   English Title: *Like Water for Chocolate*
   Author: Laura Esquivel, Mexican

8. La casa de los espíritus
   English Title: *The House of the Spirits*
   Author: Isabel Allende, Chilean

9. El último mohicano
   English Title: *The Last of the Mohicans*

10. La letra escarlata
    English Title: *The Scarlet Letter*

11. Un saco de huesos
    English Title: *Bag of Bones*

12. Mujercitas
    English Title: *Little Women*

13. Mike Mulligan y su máquina maravillosa
    English Title: *Mike Mulligan and His Marvelous Steam Shovel*

14. El parque jurásico
    Jurassic Park

Part Two *go*Spanish

Lección Quince - Unos refranes comunes

1. Hay más tiempo que vida.
   Literal translation: *There's more time than (there is) life.*

2. Del dicho al hecho hay mucho trecho.
   It's easier said than done.
   Literal translation: *Between saying something and doing it, there's a big gap.*

3. El que madruga, Dios le ayuda.
   The early bird gets the worm.
   Literal translation: *He who gets up early, God helps.*

4. Más vale llegar tarde que nunca.
   Better late than never.
   Literal translation: *It's better to arrive late than never.*

5. Ojos que no ven, corazón que no siente.
   What the eye doesn't see, the heart doesn't grieve over.
   Literal translation: *Eyes that don't see, heart that doesn't feel.*

6. Dime con quién andas y te diré quién eres.
   You're known by the company you keep.
   Literal translation: *Tell me who you are with and I'll tell you who you are.*

Part Two *go***Spanish**

Lesson Fifteen - Some Common Proverbs (cont.)

7. Panza llena, corazón contento.
   The way to a man's heart is through his stomach.
   Literal translation: *A full stomach, a happy heart.*

8. Él que no oye consejo, no llega a viejo.
   Literal translation: *He who doesn't listen to advice won't reach old age.*

9. Lo barato sale caro.
   If you buy cheaply, you pay dearly.
   Literal translation: *The inexpensive ends up being expensive.*

10. En gustos no hay disgustos.
    To each his own.
    Literal translation: *In tastes there are no arguments.*

11. El mundo es un pañuelo.
    It's a small world.
    Literal translation: *The world is a handkerchief.*

12. Mi casa es su casa.
    Make yourself at home.
    Literal translation: *My house is your house.*

Part Two *go*Spanish

Lección Dieciséis - Más refranes comunes

1. El que escupe para arriba, en la cara le cae.
   People in glass houses shouldn't throw stones.
   Literal translation: *He who looks up and spits, it will come down on his face.*

2. No te ahogues en un vaso de agua.
   Don't make a mountain out of a molehill.
   Literal translation: *Don't drown in a glass of water.*

3. Perro ladrador, poco mordedor.
   Barking dogs don't bite. / His bark is worse than his bite.
   Literal translation: *Dog barker, little biter.*

4. Quien mucho abarca, poco aprieta.
   A bird in hand is worth two in the bush.
   Literal translation: *He who grasps for too much, holds on to little.*

5. Ver es creer.
   Seeing is believing.

6. Hoy por ti, mañana por mí.
   One good turn deserves another.
   Literal translation: *Today for you, tomorrow for me.*

Part Two — *goSpanish*

Lesson Sixteen - More Common Proverbs (cont.)

7. Nadie puede servir a dos señores.
   No one can serve two masters.

8. A mal tiempo, buena cara.
   Let a smile be your umbrella.
   Literal translation: *To bad weather, a good face.*

9. De médico, poeta y loco, todos tenemos un poco.
   Literal translation: *Physician, poet, and lunatic, we all have a little of each.*

10. Querer es poder.
    Where there's a will, there's a way.
    Literal translation: *To desire is to be able to.*

11. A manos frías, corazón ardiente.
    Cold hands, warm heart.
    Literal translation: *For cold hands, a burning heart.*

12. Dinero llama a dinero.
    Money begets money.
    Literal translation: *Money calls money.*

goSpanish
Speak & Read the Pimsleur Way

Reading Program

PART THREE

Part Three   *go*Spanish
TABLE OF CONTENTS

Reading Lessons

Lección Uno: Música latinos 95
Lección Dos: La ropa 97
Lección Tres: El alfabeto 99
Lección Quatro: Las tildes 101
Lección Cinco: En el aeropuerto 103
Lección Seis: En la autopista............................. 105
Lección Siete: En el baño................................... 107
Lección Ocho: En una emergencia 109
Lección Nuevo: De viaje 111
Lección Diez: En el supermercado..................... 113
Lección Once: En el hotel 115
Lección Doce: En el restaurante......................... 117
Lección Trece: En el correo................................ 119
Lección Catorce: En el banco.............................. 121
Lección Quince: En la farmacia 123
Lección Dieciséis: En la librería 125
Lección Deicisiet: Una llamada telefónica 127
Lección Deiciocho: En una tienda de
    departmentos.. 129
Lección Deicinove: En un parque nacional......... 131
Lección Veinti: En el centro comercial 133

Part Three   *go*Spanish

Lección Uno - Música latinos

Bailes latinos / Latin Dances (1-9)

1. bolero
2. merengue
3. tango
4. mambo
5. salsa
6. samba
7. danzón
8. chachachá
9. rumba
10. cumbia
    a Colombian musical style and folk dance whose origins are African and Amerindian
11. quebradita
    a type of Mexican dance music popular in the north of Mexico

Part Three
Lesson One - Latin Music (cont.)

12. ranchera
    a type of Mexican folk song

13. plena
    a traditional form of Puerto Rican music that combines Spanish, African, and Taino music

14. son
    traditional Cuban music with origins in Africa and Spain

Part Three

*go*Spanish

Lección Dos - La ropa

1. las pantaletas
2. el sostén
3. la blusa
4. la falda
5. las medias
6. los zapatos de tacón
7. la pañoleta
8. el sombrero
9. los calzoncillos
10. la camiseta
11. la camisa
12. los pantalones
13. los calcetines
14. los zapatos
15. la corbata
16. las gafas de sol

Part Three

*go*Spanish

Lesson Two - Clothing

1. women's underpants
2. bra
3. blouse
4. skirt
5. stockings
6. high heels
7. scarf
8. hat
9. men's underpants
10. undershirt or T-shirt
11. shirt
12. pants
13. socks
14. shoes
15. tie
16. sunglasses

Part Three

goSpanish

Lección Tres - El alfabeto

1. A B C D E

2. beca
   scholarship

3. F G H I J

4. hija
   daughter

5. K L M N Ñ O

6. amigo
   friend (m)

7. P Q R S T

8. picante
   spicy, hot

9. U V W X Y Z

10. cervezas
    beers

11. Señorita
    Miss

12. Srta.

Part Three

*go*Spanish

Lesson Three - The Alphabet (continued)

13. derecha
    right

14. der.

15. izquierda
    left

16. izq.

17. Que en paz descanse.
    Rest in Peace

18. qepd
    R.I.P.

19. Estados Unidos
    United States

20. EE. UU.
    U.S.

Part Three

goSpanish

Lección Quatro - Las tildes

1. á

2. é

3. ó

4. aquí
   here

5. ñ

6. cañón
   canyon or *cannon*

7. ch

8. chica
   girl

9. ll l

10. llegó
    you / he / she / it arrived

11. rr r

12. horror
    horror

Part Three

*go***Spanish**

Lesson Four - Accent Marks (continued)

13. La señora María Bayer de Núñez
    Mrs. María Bayer de Núñez

14. señora
    Mrs.

15. María

16. Núñez

17. de Núñez
    Literal translation: *of Núñez*

18. Rodolfo Chamorro López

19. Chamorro

20. Edificio El Norte, Apartamento 15Y
    North Side Building, Apartment 15Y

21. Villeta

22. Colombia, S.A.

Part Three   *go***Spanish**

Lección Cinco - En el aeropuerto

1. Inmigración
2. Aduana
3. Información
4. Vuelos nacionales
5. Vuelos internacionales
6. Llegadas
7. Salidas
8. Transporte terrestre
9. los impuestos de salida
10. los extranjeros
11. los nacionales
12. los pasajeros
13. Estacionamiento
14. Alquiler de autos

Part Three

*go*Spanish

Lesson Five - At the Airport

1. Immigration
2. Customs
3. Information
4. Domestic Flights
5. International Flights
6. Arrivals
7. Departures
8. Ground Transportation
9. exit taxes
10. foreigners
11. citizens
12. passengers
13. Parking
14. Car Rental

Part Three

*go*Spanish

Lección Seis - En la autopista

1. el señal de alto / Pare
2. Ceda el paso
3. Despacio — Zona escolar
4. el límite de velocidad
5. el semáforo
6. el desvío
7. el agente de policía
8. la multa
9. Pase con cuidado — Reparaciones
10. Cuidado — Trabajadores en la carretera
11. Peligro — Zona de derrumbes
12. la gasolinera
13. Doble vía
14. Una vía
15. No entre
16. Prohibido estacionarse aquí

Part Three — *go*Spanish

Lesson Six - On the Highway

1. stop sign / Stop
2. Yield
3. Slow — School Zone
4. speed limit
5. traffic light
6. detour
7. police officer
8. fine
9. Proceed with Caution — Repairs
10. Caution — Workers in the Road
11. Danger — Landslide Area
12. gas station
13. Two Way
14. One Way
15. Do Not Enter.
16. No Parking (here)

Part Three *go*Spanish
Lección Siete - En el baño

1. el cepillo de dientes
2. la pasta dental — tamaño familiar
3. la seda dental
4. el jabón perfumado
5. la crema humectante
6. el papel higiénico, extra suave
7. el enchufe para rasuradora
8. la caja de klínex
9. la crema de afeitar
10. No tome agua del grifo.
11. El agua caliente en la ducha sólo dura cinco minutos.
12. Por favor no use las toallas para limpiarse el maquillaje.

Part Three

goSpanish

Lesson Seven - In the Bathroom

1. toothbrush
2. toothpaste — family size
3. dental floss
4. perfumed soap
5. moisturizing cream
6. toilet paper, super soft
7. electrical outlet for razor
8. box of Kleenex®
9. shaving cream
10. Don't drink water from the tap.
11. The hot water in the shower lasts only five minutes.
12. Please do not use the towels to remove your makeup.

Part Three   goSpanish

Lección Ocho - En una emergencia

1. Primeros auxilios
2. la ambulancia privada
3. la Clínica San Juan de Dios
4. la sala de urgencias
5. el enfermero de turno
6. el especialista
7. el seguro médico
8. la receta médica
9. el suero para reacción alérgica
10. las radiografías
11. dar de alta
12. los medicamentos

Part Three

*go*Spanish

Lesson Eight - In an Emergency

1. First Aid
2. private ambulance
3. San Juan de Dios Clinic
4. emergency room
5. shift nurse
6. specialist
7. medical insurance
8. medical prescription
9. serum for an allergic reaction
10. x-rays
11. to release from the hospital
12. medicines

Part Three

*go*Spanish

Lección Nuevo - De viaje

1. la terminal de autobuses
2. la estación de trenes
3. la excursión turística
4. el itinerario
5. las paradas
6. el viaje directo, sin escalas
7. Asientos reservados
8. Prohibido fumar.
9. La salida de emergencia
10. el chofer
11. el colectivo
12. la parada de taxis
13. ¿Está ocupado este asiento?
14. Por favor no saque la cabeza por la ventana.

Part Three

*go*Spanish

Lesson Nine - On a Trip

1. bus station
2. train station
3. guided tour
4. itinerary
5. stops
6. express trip, non-stop
7. Reserved Seating
8. No Smoking
9. Emergency Exit
10. driver
11. minibus
12. taxi stand
13. Is this seat taken?
14. Please do not put your head out the window.

Part Three   goSpanish

Lección Diez - En el supermercado

1. la entrada
2. las verduras
3. las frutas
4. quinientos gramos
5. la carne
6. el pollo
7. el pescado
8. los productos lácteos
9. los refrescos
10. los productos congelados
11. Panadería y pastelería
12. los enlatados
13. ¡Las Super Ofertas de la semana!
14. la caja registradora

Part Three

*go*Spanish

Lesson Ten - At the Supermarket

1. entrance
2. greens (vegetables)
3. fruits
4. 500 grams (approximately 1 pound)
5. meat
6. chicken
7. fish
8. dairy products
9. drinks
10. frozen products
11. Bakery and Pastry Shop
12. canned goods
13. Weekly Specials!
14. cash register

Part Three

goSpanish

Lección Once - En el hotel

1. Estimados huéspedes: ¡Bienvenidos al Hotel Buena Vista!
2. un hotel de cinco estrellas
3. la recepción
4. la gerencia
5. la mesa del botones
6. Referencia rápida de servicios
7. Este ascensor sólo sube hasta el décimo piso.
8. la tarifa para una habitación con cama doble
9. Por favor no molestar.
10. El gimnasio abre a las seis de la mañana.
11. La piscina cierra a medianoche.
12. Reciba durante toda su estancia el uso gratis del campo de golf de 18 hoyos.

Part Three   *go*Spanish

Lesson Eleven - At the Hotel

1. Valued guests: Welcome to the Hotel Buena Vista!
2. a five star hotel
3. reception desk
4. management
5. bellhop's desk
6. Quick Guide to Services
7. This elevator only goes up to the tenth floor.
8. rate for a room with a double bed
9. Please do not disturb.
10. The gym opens at six in the morning.
11. The swimming pool closes at midnight.
12. Free use of our 18 hole golf course during your entire stay.

Part Three

*go*Spanish

Lección Doce - En el restaurante

1. el ambiente familiar
2. los especiales del día
3. la especialidad de la casa
4. la lista de vinos
5. los aperitivos
6. las sopas
7. las ensaladas
8. los platos principales
9. los postres
10. las bebidas
11. la cuenta
12. la propina
13. ¿Qué nos recomienda?
14. Dos platos de la especialidad, por favor.

Part Three

*go*Spanish

Lesson Twelve - At the Restaurant

1. family setting
2. today's specials
3. specialty of the house
4. wine list
5. appetizers
6. soups
7. salads
8. main dishes
9. desserts
10. drinks
11. check, bill
12. tip
13. What do you recommend to us?
14. Two orders (Literal: *plates*) of the specialty, please.

Part Three

*go***Spanish**

Lección Trece - En el correo

1. Tengo que enviar una carta ---
2. a una amiga en Boston.
3. Aquí se venden estampillas.
4. el porte para cartas
5. las tarjetas postales
6. el código postale
7. Entrega inmediata
8. Correo registrado
9. Material impreso
10. los sobres
11. la remesa
12. frágil
13. Por favor no doblar.
14. Envío con seguro postal

Part Three   *go*Spanish

Lesson Thirteen - At the Post Office

1. I have to send a letter ---
2. to a friend in Boston.
3. Stamps are sold here.
4. postage for letters
5. postcards
6. zip code
7. Special Delivery
8. Registered Mail
9. Printed Matter
10. envelopes
11. package
12. fragile
13. Please do not bend.
14. Delivery with insurance

Part Three

*go***Spanish**

Lección Catorce - En el banco

1. las cuentas corrientes
2. las cuentas de ahorros
3. la ventanilla
4. la cajera / el cajero
5. los retiros en efectivo
6. los depósitos
7. los giros bancarios
8. la moneda nacional
9. los tipos de interés
10. las hipotecas
11. el guardia
12. las monedas
13. los billetes
14. la caja fuerte

Part Three

*go*Spanish

Lesson Fourteen - At the Bank

1. checking accounts
2. savings accounts
3. the window
4. teller (f / m)
5. cash withdrawals
6. deposits
7. bank drafts
8. local currency
9. interest rates
10. mortgages
11. guard
12. coins
13. bills
14. safe

Part Three

goSpanish

Lección Quince - En la farmacia

1. un farmacéutico / una farmacéutica
2. un laxante
3. un medicamento contra la diarrea
4. un jarabe contra la tos
5. una curita
6. un desinfectante
7. una aspirina
8. un termómetro en Fahrenheit / centígrados
9. un analgésico
10. unos productos de aseo personal
11. unos antibióticos
12. un descongestivo nasal
13. una crema antiinflamatoria
14. un antiácido

Part Three   *go*Spanish
Lesson Fifteen - At the Drugstore

1. pharmacist (m / f)
2. laxative
3. anti-diarrheal medicine
4. cough syrup
5. band-aid
6. disinfectant
7. aspirin
8. Fahrenheit / Centigrade thermometer
9. pain medicine
10. personal hygiene items
    (a generic term that encompasses all items related to bathing and cleaning of the body: soaps, shampoos, nail-cutters, deodorants, etc.)
11. antibiotics
12. nasal decongestant
13. anti-inflammatory cream
14. antacid

Part Three

Lección Dieciséis - En la librería

1. los periódicos
2. los diarios
3. los semanarios
4. las revistas
5. los libros empastados
6. los libros a la rústica
7. la guía turística
8. el mapa vial
9. la tarjeta de cumpleaños
10. los bolígrafos
11. el descuento del quince por ciento
12. los útiles de escritorio
13. el diccionario español - inglés
14. los lápices de colores
15. los carteles
16. la calculadora

Part Three

goSpanish

Lesson Sixteen - In the Bookstore

1. newspapers
2. daily newspapers
3. weekly newspapers
4. magazines
5. hardcover books
6. paperback books
7. tourist guide
8. street map
9. birthday card
10. ballpoint pens
11. 15% off
12. stationery supplies
13. a Spanish-English dictionary
14. colored pencils
15. posters
16. calculator

Part Three *go*Spanish

Lección Deicisiete - Una llamada telefónica

1. la guía telefónica
2. las páginas amarillas
3. el teléfono público
4. la llamada de larga distancia
5. el operador / la operadora
6. la tarjeta de llamadas prepagada
7. las tarifas bajas
8. la conexión mala
9. la llamada internacional
10. Ha marcado un número equivocado.
11. Por favor, cuelgue y vuelva a marcar.
12. La línea está ocupada.
13. En caso de urgencia, marque el 01.
14. Por favor deje su mensaje después del tono.

Part Three   *go*Spanish

Lesson Seventeen - A Phone Call

1. telephone book
2. yellow pages
3. pay phone
4. long distance call
5. operator (m / f)
6. prepaid phone card
7. low rates
8. bad connection
9. international call
10. You have dialed a wrong number.
11. Please hang up and dial again.
12. The line is busy.
13. In case of emergency, dial 01.
14. Please leave a message after the tone.

Part Three   goSpanish

Lección Deiciocho - En una tienda de departamentos

1. Se aceptan tarjetas de crédito.
2. Se vende
3. al contado
4. Realización: ¡Rebaja del veinticinco por ciento!
5. la ferretería
6. los juguetes
7. los electrodomésticos
8. el calzado
9. los artículos deportivos
10. la mueblería
11. Ropa para damas / caballeros
12. el recibo
13. los impuestos
14. ¡Artículos de las mejores marcas y a los mejores precios!

Part Three

*go*Spanish

Lesson Eighteen - In a Department Store

1. Credit cards accepted.
2. For Sale
3. cash sale
4. Bargain sale: Reduced 25%!
5. hardware
6. toys
7. electrical appliances
8. footwear
9. sports items
10. furniture
11. Women's / Men's Department
12. receipt
13. taxes
14. The best brands at the best prices!

Part Three   *go*Spanish

Lección Deicinove - En un parque nacional

1. Por favor no bote basura.
2. Vista panorámica
3. Las giras turísticas comienzan cada hora.
4. No se permite acampar.
5. Sitio histórico
6. Por favor, proteja el medio ambiente.
7. Agua potable
8. Se prohíbe hacer hogueras.
9. Prohibido el paso de vehículos.
10. Zona de natación
11. No hay salvavidas en esta playa.
12. Por favor no moleste a los animales.
13. Alquiler de bicicletas
14. Horario del museo

Part Three

*go*Spanish

Lesson Nineteen - At a National Park

1. Please don't litter.
2. Scenic View
3. Tours start every hour.
4. No camping allowed.
5. Historic Site
6. Please preserve our environment.
7. Drinking Water
8. Campfires prohibited.
9. No vehicles allowed.
10. Swimming Area
11. No lifeguard on this beach.
12. Please don't bother the animals.
13. Bicycle Rentals
14. Museum hours

Part Three

goSpanish

Lección Veinti - En el centro comercial

1. Vámonos de compras.
2. el directorio
3. la joyeria
4. la sala de cine
5. los baños
6. el parque de comida rápida
7. la boutique
8. la casa de música
9. la tienda de regalos
10. Prohibido montar en bicicleta.
11. la tienda de descuentos
12. No se pierda el desfile de modas a las 6 de la tarde.
13. ¿Cuánto cuesta, todo junto?
14. Es muy caro.

Part Three

*go*Spanish

Lesson Twenty - At the Mall

1. Let's go shopping.
2. store directory
3. jewelry store
4. movie theater
5. restrooms
6. food court
7. boutique
8. music store
9. gift shop
10. No bike riding.
11. discount store
12. Don't miss the fashion show at 6 P.M.
13. How much does it cost altogether?
14. It's very expensive.

Pimsleur® Language Programs are available in all
of the commonly spoken languages.

Programs in many other languages are also available.
For more information, call 1-800-831-5497
or visit us at www.Pimsleur.com

Notes

PIMSLEUR'S SPANISH LANGUAGE PROGRAMS FOR ADULTS

● ●

Spanish Comprehensive, Level I

Learn to Speak and Understand Latin American Spanish
This Edition : Compact Disk
ISBN: 9780743523578
Our Price: $345.00 U.S.

(16 CDs) 16 hours of instruction - thirty 30-minute lessons with either Culture Notes or Reading Lessons. Designed for those who want to gain fluency with 400-500 vocabulary words and several hundred sentence structures.

Notes

PIMSLEUR'S SPANISH LANGUAGE PROGRAMS FOR ADULTS

● ●

Spanish Comprehensive, Level II

Learn to Speak and Understand Latin American Spanish
This Edition : Compact Disk
ISBN: 9780743528931
Our Price: $345.00 U.S.

(16 CDs) An additional 16 hours of instruction. Designed to be used after Level I. Level II builds on Level I with 30 additional 30-minute lessons, plus Reading Lessons or Culture Notes.

For those who wish to expand their vocabulary and increase fluency.

Notes

PIMSLEUR'S SPANISH LANGUAGE PROGRAMS FOR ADULTS

● ●

Spanish Comprehensive, Level III

Learn to Speak and Understand Latin American Spanish
This Edition : Compact Disk
ISBN: 9780743528955
Our Price: $345.00 U.S.

(16 CDs) An additional 16 hours of instruction. Designed to be used after Level II. Builds on Levels I and II, with 30 additional 30-minute lessons, plus Reading Lessons or Culture Notes.

For those who wish to expand their vocabulary and increase fluency to an even higher level.

Notes

PIMSLEUR'S SPANISH LANGUAGE PROGRAMS FOR ADULTS

• •

Spanish Compact Plus

Learn to Speak and Understand Latin American Spanish
This Edition : Compact Disk
ISBN: 9780743505031
Our Price: $115.00 U.S.

(5 CDs) An additional five hours of instruction. Designed to be used after Level III. Builds on Levels I, II, and III, with 10 additional 30-minute lessons.

The Plus Program puts your language skills to the test with real-life situations. Includes a more interpersonal exchange of language at a higher level, using diverse language strategies.

PIMSLEUR'S SPANISH LANGUAGE PROGRAMS FOR CHILDREN

● ●

Speak Spanish with Dora & Diego: ¡Vamanos! Let's Go!

Learn to Speak and Understand Latin American Spanish
This Edition : Compact Disk
ISBN: 9780743599771
Our Price: $14.99 U.S.

(Two 60-minute story CDs) *Speak Spanish with Dora & Diego* is the first language course series developed that combines Dora's "can do" personality and Pimsleur's proven success at teaching languages. Includes four stories plus traditional Spanish songs on two CDs.

Set in Dora's world, it is sure to appeal to parents and children everywhere.

For children 2-6

PIMSLEUR'S SPANISH LANGUAGE PROGRAMS FOR CHILDREN

• •

Speak Spanish with Dora & Diego: Family Adventures!

Learn to Speak and Understand Latin American Spanish
This Edition : Compact Disk
ISBN: 9780743599788
Our Price: $14.99 U.S.

(Two 60-minute story CDs) *Speak Spanish with Dora & Diego* is the first language course series developed that combines Dora's "can do" personality and Pimsleur's proven success at teaching languages. Includes four stories plus traditional Spanish songs on two CDs.

Set in Dora's world, it is sure to appeal to parents and children everywhere.

For children 2-6

PIMSLEUR'S ENGLISH FOR SPANISH SPEAKERS LANGUAGE PROGRAMS

• •

Comprehensive English, Level I

Learn to Speak and Understand English as a Second Language with Pimsleur Language Programs
This Edition : Compact Disk
ISBN: 9780671784768
Our Price: $345.00 U.S.

Comprehensive English I includes 30 lessons of essential grammar and vocabulary -- 16 hours of real-life spoken practice sessions -- plus an introduction to reading.

Upon completion of this Level I program, you will have functional spoken proficiency with the most-frequently-used vocabulary and grammatical structures.

PIMSLEUR'S ENGLISH FOR SPANISH SPEAKERS LANGUAGE PROGRAMS

● ●

Inglés Integral, Nivel I

Aprenda a hablar y a entender inglés como segundo idioma con los Programas Pimsleur
Esta edición: CD
ISBN: 9780671784768
Nuestro precio: $345.00 U.S.

Inglés Integral I incluye 30 lecciones de gramática y vocabulario esenciales —16 horas de sesiones de práctica de diálogos de la vida real— más una introducción a la lectura.

Al completar este programa del Nivel I, contará con un dominio funcional del idioma hablado con el vocabulario y las estructuras gramaticales que más a menudo se usan en la vida real.

PIMSLEUR'S ENGLISH FOR SPANISH SPEAKERS LANGUAGE PROGRAMS

Comprehensive English, Level II

Learn to Speak and Understand English as a Second Language with Pimsleur Language Programs
This Edition : Compact Disk
ISBN: 9780671776251
Our Price: $345.00 U.S.

Comprehensive English II includes 30 additional lessons (16 hrs.), plus Readings, which build upon the language skills acquired in Level I. Increased spoken and reading language ability.

Level II will double your vocabulary and grammatical structures while increasing your spoken proficiency exponentially.

PIMSLEUR'S ENGLISH FOR SPANISH SPEAKERS LANGUAGE PROGRAMS

Inglés Integral, Nivel II

Aprenda a hablar y a entender inglés como segundo idioma con los Programas Pimsleur
Esta edición: CD
ISBN: 9780671776251
Nuestro precio: $345.00 U.S.

Inglés Integral II incluye 30 lecciones más (16 horas), más las lecturas, que avanzan a partir del las destrezas lingüísticas adquiridas en el Nivel I. Mayor aptitud en el lenguaje hablado y leído.

En el Nivel II duplicará su vocabulario y la cantidad de estructuras gramaticales que sabe, al tiempo que aumenta en forma exponencial sus aptitudes habladas.

PIMSLEUR'S ENGLISH FOR SPANISH SPEAKERS LANGUAGE PROGRAMS

● ●

Comprehensive English, Level I

Learn to Speak and Understand English as a Second Language with Pimsleur Language Programs
This Edition : Compact Disk
ISBN: 9780743505321
Our Price: $345.00 U.S.

Comprehensive English III includes 30 additional lessons (16 hrs.), plus Readings, which build upon the language skills acquired in Levels I and II. Increased spoken and reading language ability.

Level III will increase your vocabulary and grammatical structures and triple your spoken proficiency.

PIMSLEUR'S ENGLISH FOR SPANISH SPEAKERS LANGUAGE PROGRAMS

• •

Inglés Integral, Nivel III

Aprenda a hablar y a entender inglés como segundo idioma con los Programas Pimsleur
Esta edición: CD
ISBN: 9780743505321
Nuestro precio: $345.00 U.S.

Inglés Integral III incluye 30 lecciones más (16 horas), más las lecturas, que avanzan a partir de las destrezas adquiridas en los Niveles I y II. Mayor capacidad para manejar el idioma hablado y leído.

En el Nivel III incrementará su vocabulario y las estructuras gramaticales que sabe, y triplicará su dominio del idioma hablado.

Pimsleur programs are also available in the following languages:

- Albanian
- Arabic (Eastern)
- Arabic (Egyptian)
- Armenian (Eastern)
- Armenian (Western)
- Chinese (Cantonese)
- Chinese (Mandarin)
- Croatian
- Czech
- Danish
- Dari (Persian)
- Dutch
- Farsi (Persian)
- French
- German
- Greek
- Haitian Creole
- Hebrew
- Hindi
- Hungarian
- Indonesian
- Irish
- Italian
- Japanese
- Korean
- Lithuanian
- Norwegian
- Ojibwe
- Polish
- Portuguese (Brazilian)
- Portuguese (European)
- Romanian
- Russian
- Spanish *(for Children & Adults)*
- Swahili
- Swedish
- Swiss German
- Tagalog
- Thai
- Turkish
- Twi
- Ukrainian
- Urdu
- Vietnamese

English as a Second Language (ESL) programs are available for native-speakers of the following languages:

- Arabic
- Chinese (Cantonese)
- Chinese (Mandarin)
- Farsi (Persian)
- French
- German
- Haitian Creole
- Hindi
- Italian
- Korean
- Portuguese
- Russian
- Spanish
- Vietnamese